I0020899

Instant Heat Maps in R How-to

Learn how to design heat maps in R to enhance your data analysis

Sebastian Raschka

PUBLISHING

BIRMINGHAM - MUMBAI

Instant Heat Maps in R How-to

Copyright © 2013 Packt Publishing

All rights reserved. No part of this book may be reproduced, stored in a retrieval system, or transmitted in any form or by any means, without the prior written permission of the publisher, except in the case of brief quotations embedded in critical articles or reviews.

Every effort has been made in the preparation of this book to ensure the accuracy of the information presented. However, the information contained in this book is sold without warranty, either express or implied. Neither the author, nor Packt Publishing, and its dealers and distributors will be held liable for any damages caused or alleged to be caused directly or indirectly by this book.

Packt Publishing has endeavored to provide trademark information about all of the companies and products mentioned in this book by the appropriate use of capitals. However, Packt Publishing cannot guarantee the accuracy of this information.

First published: June 2013

Production Reference: 1180613

Published by Packt Publishing Ltd.
Livery Place
35 Livery Street
Birmingham B3 2PB, UK.

ISBN 978-1-78216-564-4

www.packtpub.com

Credits

Author
Sebastian Raschka

Reviewers
John B. Johnston
Kristopher Opron

Acquisition Editor
Martin Bell

Commissioning Editor
Yogesh Dalvi

Technical Editor
Ankita R. Meshram

Project Coordinator
Akash Poojary

Proofreader
Paul Hindle

Production Coordinator
Nitesh Thakur

Cover Work
Nitesh Thakur

Cover Image
Aditi Gajjar

About the Author

Sebastian Raschka is a PhD student at Michigan State University and is pursuing a doctorate in Biochemistry and Computer Science. He works in the field of protein structure modeling and is focused on the specificity of protein-ligand interactions. His research involves the development of a protein-ligand docking software based on a novel approach, where he combines the fields of machine learning, pattern recognition, and data mining.

In his free time, Sebastian works on web development and uses JavaScript among other technologies to develop web applications that are used by Bioinformaticians and Computational Biologists.

About the Reviewers

John Johnston is the Bioinformatics Domain Specialist for the Institute for Cyber-enabled Research at Michigan State University. He specializes in scientific analysis in a high-performance computing environment, and the development of software for the interpretation of biological data. He is an experienced Linux systems administrator and scientific consultant. He previously worked for 18 years as a Senior Groundwater Scientist for several prominent engineering firms, where he specialized in the delineation and mitigation of environmental contamination and site restoration.

Kristopher Opron is a PhD student at Michigan State University studying Computational and Mathematical Biology. For his undergraduate research, he worked under Professor Zachary Burton on molecular dynamics simulations of RNA polymerase II. He is currently working on the development of new computational tools for scientists under Professor Guowei Wei.

www.PacktPub.com

Support files, eBooks, discount offers and more

You might want to visit www.PacktPub.com for support files and downloads related to your book.

Did you know that Packt offers eBook versions of every book published, with PDF and ePub files available? You can upgrade to the eBook version at www.PacktPub.com and as a print book customer, you are entitled to a discount on the eBook copy. Get in touch with us at service@packtpub.com for more details.

At www.PacktPub.com, you can also read a collection of free technical articles, sign up for a range of free newsletters and receive exclusive discounts and offers on Packt books and eBooks.

http://PacktLib.PacktPub.com

Do you need instant solutions to your IT questions? PacktLib is Packt's online digital book library. Here, you can access, read and search across Packt's entire library of books.

Why Subscribe?

- ▸ Fully searchable across every book published by Packt
- ▸ Copy and paste, print and bookmark content
- ▸ On demand and accessible via web browser

Free Access for Packt account holders

If you have an account with Packt at www.PacktPub.com, you can use this to access PacktLib today and view nine entirely free books. Simply use your login credentials for immediate access.

Table of Contents

Preface   **1**

Instant Heat Maps in R How-to   **5**

  Creating your first heat map in R (Simple)   5

  Reading data from different file formats (Intermediate)   14

  Customizing heat maps (Intermediate)   24

  Drawing choropleth maps and contour plots (Intermediate)   33

  Exporting for presentation (Simple)   44

  Bringing your data to life (Advanced)   52

Preface

This book is about the construction of heat maps using the popular statistical programming language R. Heat maps are valuable tools for exploratory data analyses in many different applications, such as gene expression levels or stock market data. Together with powerful clustering methods, heat maps are being used to visually detect interesting patterns at one glance, even in very large data sets with hundreds of variables.

This book is a hands-on guide to provide you with a practical approach to construct such powerful heat maps. You will explore the advanced features of heat maps step-by-step, and detailed explanations on the underlying code at the end of each recipe will provide you with enough information to frame those heat maps as per your needs.

What this book covers

Creating your first heat map in R (Simple) will help you create your first heat maps from a small data set provided in R. You will use different heat map functions in R to get a first impression of their functionalities.

Reading data from different file formats (Intermediate) will help you learn how to read data from various popular file formats. After you have created your first heat maps, it is important to learn how to get your own data into R using differently formatted datasets.

Customizing heat maps (Intermediate) will help you explore more advanced functions to customize the layout of the heat maps. The main focus lies on the usage of different color palettes, but we will also cover other useful features, such as cell notes that will be used in this recipe.

Drawing choropleth maps and contour plots (Intermediate) will help you learn to create choropleth maps of the United States and other countries. Choropleth maps are a great way to visualize data from different regions on a geographical map. Also, you will learn how to visualize a 3D surface using a contour plot.

Exporting for presentation (Simple) will help you export heat maps in various popular image formats. By comparing images with different resolutions and file sizes, you will learn how to find the best-suited format for presenting your heat map.

Bringing your data to life (Advanced) will help you learn how to manipulate heat map image files to add interactivity, such as mouse-over and hover effects and fading in of supporting information.

What you need for this book

To ensure that the scripts can be used effectively, it is recommended to have a recent version of R (2.15.0 or higher) installed on your computer.

For the last recipe, a modern web browser, such as Google Chrome, Internet Explorer 10, or Safari, will be required to visualize the interactive heat maps. Note that recent versions of Firefox (18.0 or higher) have problems with the optional zoom and panning features of the interactive heat maps.

Who this book is for

This book is great for researchers and scientists, who want to make use of this free and great open source software to get the most out of their data analysis. It is recommended that you have at least some experience in using R and know how to run basic scripts from the command line. However, knowledge of other statistical scripting languages, such as Octave, S-Plus, or MATLAB, will suffice to follow through the recipes.

A strong background in Statistics is not required.

Conventions

In this book, you will find a number of styles of text that distinguish between different kinds of information. Here are some examples of these styles, and an explanation of their meaning.

Code words in text, database table names, folder names, filenames, file extensions, pathnames, dummy URLs, user input, and Twitter handles are shown as follows: "To add tool tips to our heat map, the `HeatModSVG` program will prompt us for a data file in addition to the SVG file that we want to modify."

A block of code is set as follows:

```
if (!require("gplots")) {
install.packages("gplots", dependencies = TRUE)
library(gplots)
}
```

```
if (!require("MASS")) {
install.packages("MASS", dependencies = TRUE)
library(MASS)
}
```

When we wish to draw your attention to a particular part of a code block, the relevant lines or items are set in bold:

```
-- "t" for tab
-- "c" for comma
: c
Column names? (y/n): y
Row names? (y/n): n

Read in data from car_data.csv:
```

Any command-line input or output is written as follows:

```
update.packages("gplots")

update.packages("lattice")
```

New terms and **important words** are shown in bold. Words that you see on the screen, in menus or dialog boxes for example, appear in the text like this: "First, the program asks us whether we want to add **Tool Tips** or **Zoom and Panning** or both."

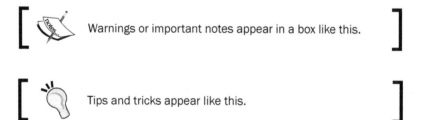

Warnings or important notes appear in a box like this.

Tips and tricks appear like this.

Reader feedback

Feedback from our readers is always welcome. Let us know what you think about this book—what you liked or may have disliked. Reader feedback is important for us to develop titles that you really get the most out of.

To send us general feedback, simply send an e-mail to feedback@packtpub.com, and mention the book title via the subject of your message.

If there is a topic that you have expertise in and you are interested in either writing or contributing to a book, see our author guide on www.packtpub.com/authors.

Customer support

Now that you are the proud owner of a Packt book, we have a number of things to help you to get the most from your purchase.

Downloading the example code

You can download the example code files for all Packt books you have purchased from your account at `http://www.packtpub.com`. If you purchased this book elsewhere, you can visit `http://www.packtpub.com/support` and register to have the files e-mailed directly to you.

Errata

Although we have taken every care to ensure the accuracy of our content, mistakes do happen. If you find a mistake in one of our books—maybe a mistake in the text or the code—we would be grateful if you would report this to us. By doing so, you can save other readers from frustration and help us improve subsequent versions of this book. If you find any errata, please report them by visiting `http://www.packtpub.com/submit-errata`, selecting your book, clicking on the **errata submission form** link, and entering the details of your errata. Once your errata are verified, your submission will be accepted and the errata will be uploaded on our website, or added to any list of existing errata, under the Errata section of that title. Any existing errata can be viewed by selecting your title from `http://www.packtpub.com/support`.

Piracy

Piracy of copyright material on the Internet is an ongoing problem across all media. At Packt, we take the protection of our copyright and licenses very seriously. If you come across any illegal copies of our works, in any form, on the Internet, please provide us with the location address or website name immediately so that we can pursue a remedy.

Please contact us at `copyright@packtpub.com` with a link to the suspected pirated material.

We appreciate your help in protecting our authors, and our ability to bring you valuable content.

Questions

You can contact us at `questions@packtpub.com` if you are having a problem with any aspect of the book, and we will do our best to address it.

Instant Heat Maps in R How-to

Welcome to *Instant Heat Maps in R How-to*.

Throughout this book, we will learn how to create simple and advanced heat maps, customize them, and create a nice output for presentations. We will be using data from various different file formats as input and work on our heat maps to add some interactivity to them.

We will also take a look at simple heat maps by creating a choropleth map of the United States and make a contour plot from topographical volcano data.

Creating your first heat map in R (Simple)

In this recipe, we will learn how to construct our first heat map in R from the `AirPassenger` data set, which is a standard data set included in the `data` package that is available with R distributions. For this task, we will use the `levelplot()` function from the `lattice` package and explore the enhanced features of the `gplots` package, the `heatmap.2()` function.

The following image shows one of the heat maps that we are going to create in this recipe from the total count of air passengers:

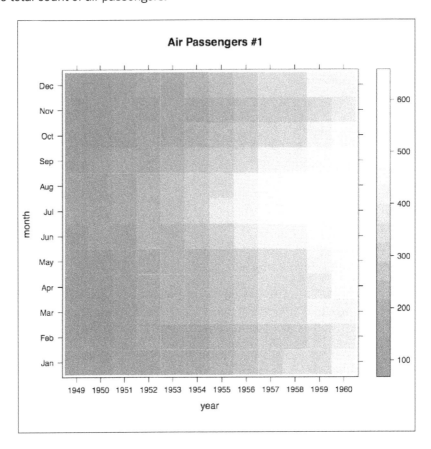

Getting ready

Download the script `5644_01_01.r` from your account at `http://www.packtpub.com` and save it to your hard disk. The first section of the script, below the comment line starting with `### loading packages`, will automatically check for the availability of the R packages `gplots` and `lattice`, which are required for this recipe.

If those packages are not already installed, you will be prompted to select an official server from the **Comprehensive R Archive Network** (**CRAN**) to allow the automatic download and installation of the required packages.

If you have already installed those two packages prior to executing the script, I recommend you to update them to the most recent version by calling the following function in the R command line:

```
update.packages("gplots")
update.packages("lattice")
```

Use the `source()` function in the R command-line to execute an external script from any location on your hard drive.

If you start a new R session from the same directory as the location of the script, simply provide the name of the script as an argument in the function call as follows:

```
source("myScript.r")
```

You have to provide the absolute or relative path to the script on your hard drive if you started your R session from a different directory to the location of the script. Refer to the following example:

```
source("/home/username/Downloads/myScript.r")
```

You can view the current working directory of your current R session by executing the following command in the R command-line:

```
getwd()
```

How to do it...

Run the `56440S_01_01.r` script in R to execute the following code, and take a look at the output printed on the screen as well as the PDF file, `first_heatmaps.pdf` that will be created by this script:

```
### loading packages
if (!require("gplots")) {
install.packages("gplots", dependencies = TRUE)
library(gplots)
}
if (!require("lattice")) {
install.packages("lattice", dependencies = TRUE)
library(lattice)
}

### loading data
data(AirPassengers)

### converting data
rowcolNames <- list(as.character(1949:1960), month.abb)
air_data <- matrix(AirPassengers,
  ncol = 12,
  byrow = TRUE,
```

```
    dimnames = rowcolNames)

### drawing heat maps
pdf("firstHeatmaps.pdf")

# 1) Air Passengers #1
print(levelplot(air_data,
  col.regions=heat.colors,
  xlab = "year",
  ylab = "month",
  main = "Air Passengers #1"))

# 2) Air Passengers #2
heatmap.2(air_data,
  trace = "none",
  density.info = "none",
  xlab = "month",
  ylab = "year",
  main = "Air Passengers #2")

# 3) Air Passengers #3
heatmap.2(air_data,
  trace = "none",
  xlab = "month",
  ylab = "year",
  main = "Air Passengers #3",
  density.info = "histogram",
  dendrogram = "column",
  keysize = 1.8)

dev.off()
```

Downloading the example code

You can download the example code files for all Packt books you have
purchased from your account at http://www.packtpub.com. If you
purchased this book elsewhere, you can visit http://www.packtpub.
com/support and register to have the files e-mailed directly to you.

How it works...

There are different functions for drawing heat maps in R, and each has its own advantages
and disadvantages. In this recipe, we will take a look at the levelplot() function from
the lattice package to draw our first heat map. Furthermore, we will use the advanced
heatmap.2() function from gplots to apply a clustering algorithm to our data and add
the resulting dendrograms to our heat maps.

The following image shows an overview of the different plotting functions that we are using throughout this book:

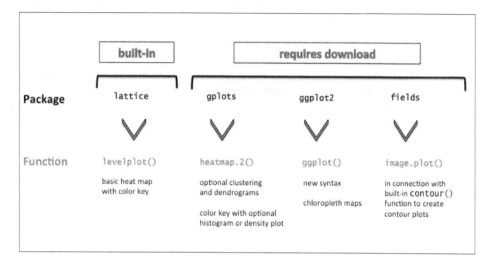

Now let us take a look at how we read in and process data from different data files and formats step-by-step:

1. **Loading packages**: The first eight lines preceding the ### loading data section will make sure that R loads the lattice and gplots package, which we need for the two heat map functions in this recipe: levelplot() and heatmap.2().

> Each time we start a new session in R, we have to load the required packages in order to use the levelplot() and heatmap.2() functions. To do so, enter the following function calls directly into the R command-line or include them at the beginning of your script:
>
> ▸ library(lattice)
> ▸ library(gplots)

2. **Loading the data set**: R includes a package called data, which contains a variety of different data sets for testing and exploration purposes. More information on the different data sets that are contained in the data package can be found at http://stat.ethz.ch/ROmanual/ROpatched/library/datasets/.

    For this recipe, we are loading the AirPassenger data set, which is a collection of the total count of air passengers (in thousands) for international airlines from 1949-1960 in a time-series format.

    ```
    data(AirPassengers)
    ```

3. **Converting the data set into a numeric matrix**: Before we can use the heat map functions, we need to convert the `AirPassenger` time-series data into a numeric matrix first. Numeric matrices in R can have characters as row and column labels, but the content itself must consist of one single mode: numerical.

   We use the `matrix()` function to create a numeric matrix consisting of 12 columns to which we pass the `AirPassenger` time-series data row-by-row. Using the argument `dimnames = rowcolNames`, we provide row and column names that we assigned previously to the variable `rowColNames`, which is a list of two vectors: a series of 12 strings representing the years 1949 to 1960, and a series of strings for the 12 three-letter abbreviations of the months from January to December, respectively.

```
rowcolNames <- list(as.character(1949:1960), month.abb)
air_data <- matrix(AirPassengers,
  ncol = 12,
  byrow = TRUE,
  dimnames = rowcolNames)
```

4. **A simple heat map using levelplot()**: Now that we have converted the `AirPassenger` data into a numeric matrix format and assigned it to the variable `air_data`, we can go ahead and construct our first heat map using the `levelplot()` function from the `lattice` package:

```
print(levelplot(air_data,
  col.regions=heat.colors,
  xlab = "year",
  ylab = "month",
  main = "Air Passengers #1"))
```

The `levelplot()` function creates a simple heat map with a color key to the right-hand side of the map. We can use the argument `col.regions = heat.colors` to change the default color transition to yellow and red. X and y axis labels are specified by the `xlab` and `ylab` parameters, respectively, and the `main` parameter gives our heat map its caption.

In contrast to most of the other plotting functions in R, the `lattice` package returns objects, so we have to use the `print()` function in our script if we want to save the plot to a data file. In an interactive R session, the `print()` call can be omitted. Typing the name of the variable will automatically display the referring object on the screen.

5. **Creating enhanced heat maps with heatmap.2()**: Next, we will use the `heatmap.2()` function to apply a clustering algorithm to the `AirPassenger` data and to add row and column dendrograms to our heat map:

```
heatmap.2(air_data,
    trace = "none",
    density.info = "none",
  xlab = "month",
  ylab = "year",
  main = "Air Passengers #2")
```

 Hierarchical clustering is especially popular in gene expression analyses. It is a very powerful method for grouping data to reveal interesting trends and patterns in the data matrix.

Another neat feature of `heatmap.2()` is that you can display a histogram of the count of the individual values inside the color key by including the argument `density.info = NULL` in the function call. Alternatively, you can set `density.info = "density"` for displaying a density plot inside the color key.

By adding the argument `keysize = 1.8`, we are slightly increasing the size of the color key—the default value of `keysize` is `1.5`:

```
heatmap.2(air_data,
  trace = "none",
  xlab = "month",
  ylab = "year",
  main = "Air Passengers #3",
density.info = "histogram",
dendrogram = "column",
  keysize = 1.8)
```

Did you notice the missing row dendrogram in the resulting heat map? This is due to the argument `dendrogram = "column"` that we passed to the heat map function. Similarly, you can type row instead of column to suppress the column dendrogram, or use neither to draw no dendrogram at all.

There's more...

By default, `levelplot()` places the color key on the right-hand side of the heat map, but it can be easily moved to the top, bottom, or left-hand side of the map by modifying the `space` parameter of `colorkey`:

```
levelplot(air_data,
col.regions = heat.colors,
colorkey = list(space = "top"))
```

Replacing `top` by `left` or `bottom` will place the color key on the left-hand side or on the bottom of the heat map, respectively.

Moving around the color key for `heatmap.2()` can be a little bit more of a hassle. In this case we have to modify the parameters of the `layout()` function. By default, `heatmap.2()` passes a matrix, `lmat`, to `layout()`, which has the following content:

```
       [,1] [,2]
 [1,]    4    3
 [2,]    2    1
```

The numbers in the preceding matrix specify the locations of the different visual elements on the plot (1 implies heat map, 2 implies row dendrogram, 3 implies column dendrogram, and 4 implies key). If we want to change the position of the key, we have to modify and rearrange those values of `lmat` that `heatmap.2()` passes to `layout()`.

For example, if we want to place the color key at the bottom left-hand corner of the heat map, we need to create a new matrix for `lmat` as follows:

```
lmat
       [,1] [,2]
 [1,]    0    3
 [2,]    2    1
 [3,]    4    0
```

We can construct such a matrix by using the `rbind()` function and assigning it to `lmat`:

```
lmat = rbind(c(0,3),c(2,1),c(4,0))
```

Furthermore, we have to pass an argument for the column height parameter `lhei` to `heatmap.2()`, which will allow us to use our modified `lmat` matrix for rearranging the color key:

```
heatmap.2(air_data,
dendrogram = "none",
trace = "none",
density.info = "none",
keysize = "1.3",
xlab = "month",
ylab = "year",
main = "Air Passengers",
lmat = rbind(c(0,3),c(2,1),c(4,0)),
lhei = c(1.5,4,1.5))
```

If you don't need a color key for your heat map, you could turn it off by using the argument `key = FALSE` for `heatmap.2()` and `colorkey = FALSE` for `levelplot()`, respectively.

R also has a base function for creating heat maps that does not require you to install external packages and is most advantageous if you can go without a color key. The syntax is very similar to the `heatmap.2()` function, and all options for `heatmap.2()` that we have seen in this recipe also apply to `heatmap()`:

```
heatmap(air_data,
    xlab = "month",
    ylab = "year",
    main = "Air Passengers")
```

More information on dendrograms and clustering

By default, the dendrograms of `heatmap.2()` are created by a **hierarchical agglomerate clustering** method, also known as **bottom-up clustering**.

In this approach, all individual objects start as individual clusters and are successively merged until only one single cluster remains. The distance between a pair of clusters is calculated by the **farthest neighbor** method, also called the **complete linkage** method, which is based by default on the Euclidean distance of the two points from both clusters that are farthest apart from each other. The computed dendrograms are then reordered based on the row and column means.

By modifying the default parameters of the `dist()` function, we can use another distance measure rather than the **Euclidean distance**. For example, if we want to use the **Manhattan distance** measure (based on a grid-like path rather than a direct connection between two objects), we would modify the `method` parameter of the `dist()` function and assign it to a variable `distance` first:

```
distance = dist(myData, method = "manhattan")
```

Other options for the `method` parameter are: `euclidean` (default), `maximum`, `canberra`, `binary`, or `minkowski`.

To use other agglomeration methods than the **complete linkage** method, we modify the `method` parameter in the `hclust()` function and assign it to another variable `cluster`. Note the first argument `distance` that we pass to the `hclust()` function, which comes from our previous assignment:

```
cluster = hclust(distance, method = "ward")
```

By setting the `method` parameter to `ward`, R will use Joe H. Ward's **minimum variance** method for hierarchical clustering. Other options for the `method` parameter that we can pass as arguments to `hclust()` are: `complete` (default), `single`, `average`, `mcquitty`, `median`, or `centroid`.

To use our modified clustering parameters, we simply call the `as.dendrogram()` function within `heatmap.2()` using the variable `cluster` that we assigned previously:

```
heatmap.2(myData,
Colv = as.dendrogram(cluster),
Rowv = as.dendrogram(cluster))
```

We can also draw the cluster dendrogram without the heat map by using the `plot()` function:

```
plot(cluster)
```

To turn off row and column reordering, we need to turn off the dendrograms and set the parameters `Colv` and `Rowv` to NA:

```
heatmap.2(my_data, dendrograms = "none", Colv = "NA",
Rowv = "NA")
```

Reading data from different file formats (Intermediate)

In the previous recipe, we familiarized ourselves with heat map functions in R using built-in data. Now, we will learn how to use external data to create our heat maps.

In real life, we often have no control over the format of the data files that we download, or the data that is the output of a particular program. Because we can not always rely on luck that the data comes in the right format, we will learn in this recipe how to read in data from different file formats and get it into shape.

The following image shows a heat map that we are going to create from the `gene_expression.txt` data set in this recipe:

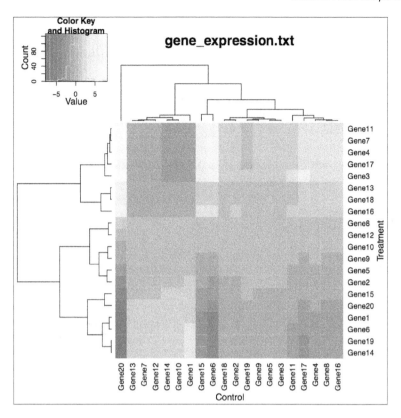

Getting ready

Download the script `56440S_02_01.r` and the data sets `gene_expression.txt`, `runners.csv`, and `apple_stocks.xlsx` from your account at `http://www.packtpub.com` and save them to your hard drive.

I recommend that you download and save the script and data files to the same folder on your hard drive. If you execute the script from a different location to the location of the data files, you have to change the current R working directory accordingly.

You can change the current working directory of your R session by using the `setwd()` function. If you saved the data files for this recipe under `/home/user/Downloads`, for example, you would type `setwd("/home/user/Downloads")` into the R command-line. Alternatively, you can uncomment the fourth line of the script and provide the location of the data file directory to the `setwd()` function in a similar way.

For more information on how to view the current working directory of your current R session and an explanation on how to run scripts in R, please read the *Getting ready* section of the *Creating your first heat map in R* recipe.

How to do it...

After you have executed the following code from the `56440S_02_01.r` script, take a look at the PDF file `readingData.pdf`, which was created in the same location where you executed the script:

```
# if you are running the script from a different location
# than the location of the data sets, uncomment the
# next line and point setwd() to the data set location
# setwd("/home/username/Datasets")

### loading packages
if (!require("gplots")) {
install.packages("gplots", dependencies = TRUE)
library(gplots)
}
if (!require("lattice")) {
install.packages("lattice", dependencies = TRUE)
library(lattice)
}
if (!require("xlsx")) {
install.packages("xlsx", dependencies = TRUE)
library(xlsx)
}

pdf("readingData.pdf")

### loading data and drawing heat maps

# 1) gene_expression.txt
gene_data <- read.table("gene_expression.txt",
  comment.char = "/",
  blank.lines.skip = TRUE,
  header = TRUE,
```

```
    sep = "\t",
    nrows = 20)
gene_data <- data.matrix(gene_data)
gene_ratio <- outer(gene_data[,"Treatment"],
    gene_data[,"Control"],
    FUN = "/")
heatmap.2(gene_ratio,
    xlab = "Control",
    ylab = "Treatment",
    trace = "none",
    main = "gene_expression.txt")

# 2) runners.csv
runner_data <- read.csv("runners.csv")
rownames(runner_data) <- runner_data[,1]
runner_data <- data.matrix(runner_data[,2:ncol(runner_data)])
colnames(runner_data) <- c(2003:2012)
runner_data[runner_data == 0.00] <- NA
heatmap.2(runner_data,
    dendrogram = "none",
    Colv = NA,
    Rowv = NA,
    trace = "none",
    na.color = "gray",
    main = "runners.csv",
    margin = c(8,10))

# 3) apple_stocks.xlsx
stocks_table <- read.xlsx("apple_stocks.xlsx",
    sheetIndex = 1,
    rowIndex = c(1:28),
    colIndex = c(1:5,7))
row_names <- (stocks_table[,1])
stocks_matrix <- data.matrix(
    stocks_table[2:ncol(stocks_table)])
rownames(stocks_matrix) <- as.character(row_names)
stocks_data = t(stocks_matrix)
print(levelplot(stocks_data,
    col.regions = heat.colors,
    margin = c(10,10),
    scales = list(x = list(rot = 90)),
    main = "apple_stocks.xlsx",
    ylab = NULL,
    xlab = NULL))

dev.off()
```

How it works...

Generally, R is able to read data from any file that contains data in a proper text format. First, we will see how to use the universal `read.table()` function to read data from a `.txt` file. Next, the recipe shows us how to read data from a **Comma Separated Values** (**CSV**) file using the `read.csv()` function. And finally, we take a look at the `xlsx()` function from the `xlsx` package, in order to process Microsoft Excel spreadsheet files.

1. **Inspecting gene_expression.txt**: The first file that reads into R, `gene_expression.txt`, contains exemplary gene expression data obtained from two different conditions: control and treatment. The individual values in this data file resemble fold-differences of gene expression relative to a housekeeping gene that was used as a reference to normalize the data.

   The data was saved as a `.txt` file and consists of 105 lines. The first two lines from the top are comments about the data and begin with a slash (/) as the first character. Followed by two blank lines, a header labels the two data columns of the expression data under the two conditions.

   Notice that the data columns are separated by tab spaces as shown in the following screenshot of the `gene_expression.txt` data set:

```
                          gene_expression.txt
/ fold changes of gene expression for 100 genes
/ in comparison to a reference gene


Control  Treatment
Gene1    -1.8361701   -3.2293547
Gene2    3.3078555    -1.4261356
...
Gene100 1.7681588     1.9091917
```

2. **Reading data from gene_expression.txt**: Let's take a look at the arguments we need to provide in the `read.table()` function in order to read this data file as a data table into R:

```
gene_data <- read.table("gene_expression.txt",
  comment.char = "/",
  blank.lines.skip = TRUE,
  header = TRUE,
  sep = "\t",
  nrows = 20)
```

When we use the `read.table()` function, R ignores every line in the data file that starts with a hash mark (#), which is the default comment character. However, the first character of the comment lines in our data file is a forward slash (/). Therefore, we have to pass it to the function as an additional argument for the `comment.char` parameter so R can interpret the first two lines in `gene_expression.txt` as comments and skip them. The second argument, `blank.lines.skip = TRUE`, ensures that R also skips the two blank lines after the comment section.

 Alternatively, we could also use the argument `skip = 4` to force R to ignore the first four lines in this text file.

From here on, R will read every line that follows and will interpret it as data—skipping the comment and blank lines at the beginning.

There are two data columns in this text file, which are labeled as `Control` and `Treatment`. By setting the header parameter to `TRUE`, R will store these labels as a header for our data table. The header is followed by 100 rows of tab-delimited data (`Gene1` to `Gene100`). We need to use the argument `sep = "/t"` to set the field separator character to a tab space, since the default data field separator is the white space, `sep = ""`.

The data file is quite large with its 100 entries, and for this example, we just use the first 20 genes to create our heat map. We can tell R to stop reading data after the 20th entry by providing the argument `nrows = 20` in the function call.

3. **Converting the data table into a numerical matrix**: As we remember from the *Creating your first heat map in R* recipe, we need to convert our data into a numeric matrix format before we can use it to create a heat map. Instead of using the relative expression measures deployed in the data file, we are interested in showing the fold-changes of the gene expression levels. To calculate those fold-changes of the `Treatment` column in relation to the `Control` column, we are using the `outer()` function. This function allows us to create a 20 x 20 matrix by dividing each gene from the `Treatment` column (third column in the data file) by each gene from the `Control` column (second column in the data file):

```
gene_data <- data.matrix(gene_data)
gene_ratio <- outer(gene_data[,"Treatment"],
  gene_data[,"Control"],
  FUN = "/")
```

4. **Reading data from runners.csv**: The `runners.csv` file contains the fastest personal times of seven popular 100 meters sprinters for the years between 2003 and 2012.

If we want to read a data file with comma-separated values, it is most convenient to use the `read.csv()` function:

```
runner_data <- read.csv("runners.csv")
```

Basically, the `read.csv()` function is a derivative of `read.table()` with the following default parameters:

```
runner_data <- read.table("runners.csv",
header = TRUE,
sep = ",", ...)
```

5. **Dealing with missing values in runners.csv**: The default constant for missing values in R is `NA`, which stands for `Not Available`. Therefore, if we read data from a file that contains empty fields, missing values will be replaced by `NA` when R creates the data table.

When we read in `runner_data.csv`, we see that our data table contains many `0.00` values, which means that no time was recorded for the runner in those years. However, it would make more sense to have those values denoted as missing data (`NA`) in our heat map.

So, if we want R to interpret values other than `NA` or empty fields as missing values, we do this by providing an argument for the `na.strings` parameter in our `read.table()` or `read.csv()` function:

```
runner_data <- read.csv("runners.csv", na.strings = 0.00)
```

We can convert also particular data in the table to missing values after we read it from a file. In our case, we could use the following command to convert all `0.00` data points to missing values:

`runner_data[runner_data == 0.00] <- NA`

By default, cells with `NA` values will be left blank and appear as white cells in our heat map. This can be very misleading, since the color palette that we are using converges into a very bright yellow. It would be very hard to distinguish those empty cells from values that are seeded very high in our color key.

To avoid this confusion, we can simply assign a different color to those cells that contain missing values. Here, we are coloring them in gray:

```
heatmap.2(runner_data,
    dendrogram = "none",
  Colv = NA,
  Rowv = NA,
```

```
    trace = "none",
    na.color = "gray",
    main = "runners.csv",
    margin = c(8,10))
```

 You can also remove all incomplete data rows—that contain at least one or more missing values—by calling the `na.omit()` function on a data table as follows:

```
    runner_data <- na.omit(runner_data)
```

6. **Reading Apple's stock data from an Excel spreadsheet file**: Now, let us take a look at Apple's daily stock market data from 1984 to 2013.

   The following screenshot shows the `apple_stock.xlsx` data set opened in Microsoft Excel 2011:

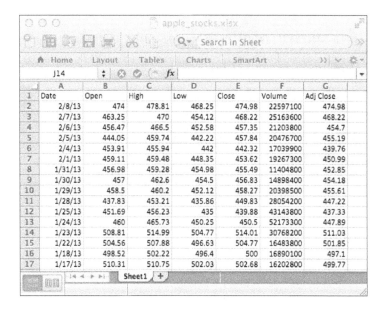

R has no in-built function to read data from this proprietary format. But, we are lucky that someone developed the `xlsx` package especially for this case that is freely available on CRAN. Therefore, we can use the `read.xlsx()` function to conveniently get this data from `apple_stock.xlsx` into R.

```
stocks_table <- read.xlsx("apple_stocks.xlsx",
    sheetIndex = 1,
    rowIndex = c(1:28),
    colIndex = c(1:5,7))
```

With `sheetIndex`, we have selected which sheet we want to read from the Excel spreadsheet file—`apple_stock.xlsx` only has data on `sheet 1`. The spreadsheet consists of 7168 rows of data, but we are interested only in the recent data stock data of 2013. So, to only read in those first 28 lines, we included the `rowIndex = c(1:28)` argument in the `read.xlsx()` function call above. Furthermore, we are not interested in the `Volume` column (column 6), so let's skip it via the argument `colIndex = c(1:5,7)`.

> You can also use the `read.xlsx()` function to read data from the old Excel spreadsheet format `.xls`.

In most cases, we will use the `read.table()` function to read our data into R. The following table summarizes the most important options:

Important **read.table()** Parameters

read.table() Parameter	Default	Arguments
header	FALSE	FALSE, TRUE
sep	" "	",", ".", "/", "\t", ...
dec	"."	".", ","
na.strings	"NA"	"0", "NaN", "0.00", "-", ...
skip	0	*positive integer*
blank.lines.skip	TRUE	TRUE, FALSE
comment.char	"#"	"/", "!", ">", ...
nrows	-1	-1, *positive integer*

There's more...

It might happen that we obtain our data in the so-called long format, which contains multiple rows for each individual category, individual or item.

To give you a better understanding, an excerpt from the `runners.csv` data set in long format is shown as follows:

```
    Year        Runner    Time
1 2007     Usain_Bolt    10.03
2 2008     Usain_Bolt    9.72
3 2009     Usain_Bolt    9.58
4 2010     Usain_Bolt    9.82
5 2011     Usain_Bolt    9.76
6 2012     Usain_Bolt    9.63
7 2004   Asafa_Powell    10.02
8 2005   Asafa_Powell    9.87
...
```

Do you see the problem here? The `Runner` column in the middle of the data table consists of character strings, which are incompatible with the numeric matrix format that is required by our heat map functions.

Fortunately, it is quite easy to convert data from long to wide format—we can simply use the cross tabulation function `xtabs()`:

```
runners_wide <- xtabs(formula = Time ~ Runner + Year, data =
runners_long))
```

```
                Year
Runner            2004    2005    2007    2008    2009    2010    2011    2012
  Asafa_Powell  10.02    9.87    0.00    0.00    0.00    0.00    0.00    0.00
  Usain_Bolt     0.00    0.00   10.03    9.72    9.58    9.82    9.76    9.63
```

> If you just want to transpose your data, that is, switch columns and rows, you can use the `t()` function:
>
> ```
> transposed_data <- t(my_data)
> ```

More information on decimal marks

Several countries use a decimal comma instead of a decimal point. Chances are high that you want to analyze a data set that comes from one of those countries. In this case you just have to provide an additional argument for the `dec` parameter:

```
my_data <- read.table("data.txt", dec=",")
```

Customizing heat maps (Intermediate)

There is always room for improvements. Now that we have seen how to create impressive heat maps from various different data file types, it is time to add some extraordinary style.

To ensure that our heat maps look good in any situation, we will make use of different color palettes in this recipe, and we will even learn how to create our own.

Further, we will add some more extras to our heat maps including visual aids such as cell note labels, which will make them even more useful and accessible as a tool for visual data analysis.

The following image shows a heat map with cell notes and an alternative color palette created from the `arabidopsis_genes.csv` data set:

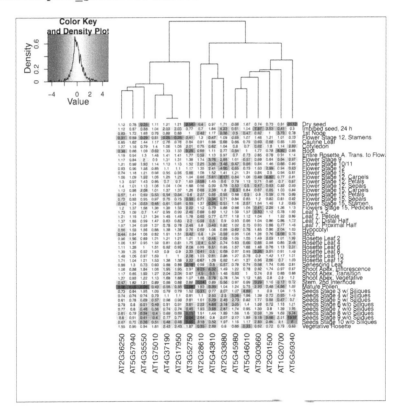

Getting ready

Download the 56440S_03_01.r script and the Arabidopsis_genes.csv data set from your account at http://www.packtpub.com and save it to your hard drive.

I recommend that you save the script and data file to the same folder on your hard drive. If you execute the script from a different location to the data file, you will have to change the current R working directory accordingly.

Please read the *Getting ready* section of the *Reading data from different data formats* recipe for more information on how to change the working directory of your current R session.

For more information on how to view the current working directory of your current R session and an explanation on how to run scripts in R, please read the *Getting ready* section of the *Creating your first heat map* recipe.

The script will check automatically if any additional packages need to be installed in R. You can find more information about the installation of packages in the *Getting ready* section of the *Creating your first heat map* recipe.

How to do it...

Execute the following code in R via the 56440S_03_01.r script and take a look at the PDF file custom_heatmaps.pdf that will be created in the current working directory:

```
### loading packages
if (!require("gplots")) {
install.packages("gplots", dependencies = TRUE)
library(RColorBrewer)
}
if (!require("RColorBrewer")) {
install.packages("RColorBrewer", dependencies = TRUE)
library(RColorBrewer)
}

### reading in data
gene_data <- read.csv("arabidopsis_genes.csv")
row_names <- gene_data[,1]
gene_data <- data.matrix(gene_data[,2:ncol(gene_data)])
rownames(gene_data) <- row_names
```

```
### setting heatmap.2() default parameters
heat2 <- function(...) heatmap.2(gene_data,
  tracecol = "black",
  dendrogram = "column",
  Rowv = NA,
  trace = "none",
  margins = c(8,10),
  density.info = "density", ...)

pdf("custom_heatmaps.pdf")

### 1) customizing colors
# 1.1) in-built color palettes
heat2(col = terrain.colors(n = 1000),
  main = "1.1) Terrain Colors")

# 1.2) RColorBrewer palettes
heat2(col = brewer.pal(n = 9, "YlOrRd"),
  main = "1.2) Brewer Palette")

# 1.3) creating own color palettes
my_colors <- c(y1 = "#F7F7D0",
  y2 = "#FCFC3A",
  y3 = "#D4D40D",
  b1 = "#40EDEA",
  b2 = "#18B3F0",
  b3 = "#186BF0",
  r1 = "#FA8E8E",
  r2 = "#F26666",
  r1 = "#C70404")
heat2(col = my_colors,
  main = "1.3) Own Color Palette")
my_palette <- colorRampPalette(c("blue", "yellow", "red"))(n = 1000)
heat2(col = my_palette, main = "1.3) ColorRampPalette")

# 1.4) gray scale
heat2(col = gray(level = (0:100)/100),
  main ="1.4) Gray Scale")

### 2) adding cell notes
fold_change <- 2^gene_data
rounded_fold_changes <- round(rounded_fold_changes, 2)
heat2(cellnote = rounded,
  notecex = 0.5,
```

```
      notecol = "black",
    col = my_palette,
    main = "2) Cell Notes")

### 3) adding column side colors
heat2(ColSideColors = c("red", "gray", "red",
rep("green",13)),
    main = "3) ColSideColors")

  dev.off()
```

How it works...

Primarily, we will be using the already familiar functions from the previous recipes, read. csv() and heatmap.2(), to read in data into R and construct our heat maps. In this recipe, however, we will focus on advanced features to enhance our heat maps, such as customizing color and other visual elements:

1. **Inspecting the arabidopsis_genes.csv data set**: The arabidopsis_genes. csv file contains a compilation of gene expression data from the model plant Arabidopsis thaliana. I obtained the freely available data of 16 different genes as log 2 ratios of target and reference gene from the Arabidopsis eFP Browser (http://bar.utoronto.ca/efp_arabidopsis/). For each gene, expression data of 47 different areas of the plant is available in this data file.

2. **Reading the data and converting it into a numeric matrix**: As we already know from the previous recipe, we have to convert the data table into a numeric matrix first before we can construct our heat maps:

```
gene_data <- read.csv("arabidopsis_genes.csv")
row_names <- gene_data[,1]
gene_data <- data.matrix(gene_data[,2:ncol(gene_data)])
rownames(gene_data) <- row_names
```

3. **Creating a customized heatmap.2() function**: To reduce typing efforts, we are defining our own version of the heatmap.2() function now, where we will include some arguments that we are planning to keep using throughout this recipe:

```
heat2 <- function(...) heatmap.2(gene_data,
    tracecol = "black",
    dendrogram = "column",
    Rowv = NA,
    trace = "none",
    margins = c(8,10),
    density.info = "density", ...)
```

So, each time we call our newly defined `heat2()` function, it will behave similar to the `heatmap.2()` function, except for the additional arguments that we will pass along. We also include a new argument, `black`, for the `tracecol` parameter, to better distinguish the density plot in the color key from the background.

4. **The built-in color palettes**: In the previous recipes, we used the default color palette of `heatmap.2()`, `heat.colors`, which represents a color transition from yellow to red. There are four more color palettes available in the base R that we could use instead of the `heat.colors` palette: `rainbow`, `terrain.colors`, `topo.colors`, and `cm.colors`.

    So let us make use of the `terrain.colors` color palette now, which will give us a nice color transition from green over yellow to rose:

    ```
    heat2(col = terrain.colors(n = 1000),
      main = "1.1) Terrain Colors")
    ```

    If you recall the heat maps that we created in the previous two recipes, you might have noticed that the transition between the colors in the color key was not really smooth, but rather abrupt. The five color palettes mentioned previously allow us to define the number of different color shades that we can use. Therefore every number for the parameter `n` that is larger than the default value 12 will add additional colors, which will make the transition smoother. A value of 1000 for the `n` parameter should be more than sufficient to make the transition between the individual colors indistinguishable to the human eye.

     You can find more information about the positioning of the color key in the *There's more...* section of the *Creating your first heat map in R* recipe.

    The following image shows a side-by-side comparison of the `heat.colors` and `terrain.colors` color palettes using a different number of color shades:

    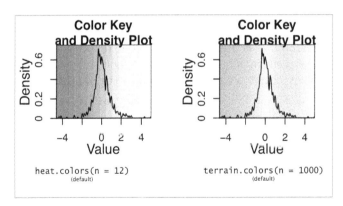

Further, it is also possible to reverse the direction of the color transition. For example, if we want to have a `heat.color` transition from yellow to red instead of red to yellow in our heat map, we could simply define a reverse function:

```
rev_heat.colors <- function(x) rev(heat.colors(x))
heat2(col = rev_heat.colors(500))
```

5. **RColorBrewer palettes**: A lot of color palettes are available from the `RColorBrewer` package. To see how they look like, you can type `display.brewer.all()` into the R command-line after loading the `RColorBrewer` package. However, in contrast to the dynamic range color palettes that we have seen previously, the `RColorBrewer` palettes have a distinct number of different colors. So to select all nine colors from the `YlOrRd` palette, a gradient from yellow to red, we use the following command:

```
heat2(col = brewer.pal(n = 9, "YlOrRd"),
  main = "1.2) Brewer Palette")
```

The following image gives you a good overview of all the different color palettes that are available from the `RColorBrewer` package:

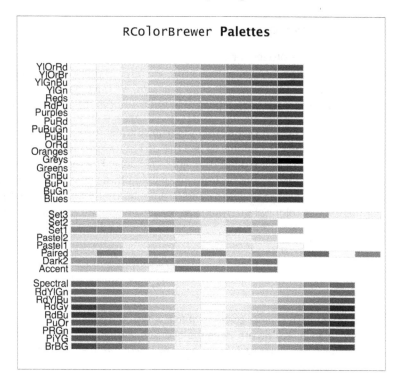

6. **Creating our own color palettes**: Next, we will see how we can create our own color palettes. A whole bunch of different colors are already defined in R. An overview of those colors can be seen by typing `colors()` into the command line of R.

   The most convenient way to assign new colors to a color palette is using **hex colors** (hexadecimal colors). Many different online tools are freely available that allow us to obtain the necessary hex codes. A great example is color picker (`http://www.colorpicker.com`), which allows us to choose from a rich color table and provides us with the corresponding hex codes.

   Once we gather all the hexadecimal codes for the colors that we want to use for our color palette, we can assign them to a variable as we have done before with the explicit color names:

   ```
   my_colors <- c(y1 = "#F7F7D0",
     y2 = "#FCFC3A",
     y3 = "#D4D40D",
     b1 = "#40EDEA",
     b2 = "#18B3F0",
     b3 = "#186BF0",
     r1 = "#FA8E8E",
     r2 = "#F26666",
     r1 = "#C70404")
   heat2(col = my_colors,
     main = "1.3) Own Color Palette")
   ```

   This is a very handy approach for creating a color key with very distinct colors. However, the downside of this method is that we have to provide a lot of different colors if we want to create a smooth color gradient; we have used 1000 different colors for the `terrain.color()` palette to get a smooth transition in the color key!

7. **Using colorRampPalette for smoother color gradients**: A convenient approach to create a smoother color gradient is to use the `colorRampPalette()` function, so we don't have to insert all the different colors manually. The function takes a vector of different colors as an argument. Here, we provide three colors: `blue` for the lower end of the color key, `yellow` for the middle range, and `red` for the higher end. As we did it for the in-built color palettes, such as `heat.color`, we assign the value 1000 to the n parameter:

   ```
   my_palette <- colorRampPalette(c("blue", "yellow", "red"))(n =
   1000)
   heat2(col = my_palette, main = "1.3) ColorRampPalette")
   ```

In this case, it is more convenient to use discrete color names over hex colors, since we are using the `colorRampPalette()` function to create a gradient and do not need all the different shades of a particular color.

8. **Grayscales**: It might happen that the medium or device that we use to display our heat maps does not support colors. Under these circumstances, we can use the `gray` palette to create a heat map that is optimized for those conditions.

   The level parameter of the `gray()` function takes a vector with values between 0 and 1 as an argument, where 0 represents black and 1 represents white, respectively. For a smooth gradient, we use a vector with 100 equally spaced shades of gray ranging from 0 to 1.

```
heat2(col = gray(level = (0:200)/200),
   main ="1.4) Gray Scale")
```

 We can make use of the same color palettes for the `levelplot()` function too. It works in a similar way as it did for the `heatmap.2()` function that we are using in this recipe. However, inside the `levelplot()` function call, we must use `col.regions` instead of the simple `col`, so that we can include a color palette argument.

9. **Adding cell notes to our heat map**: Sometimes, we want to show a data set along with our heat map. A neat way is to use so-called cell notes to display data values inside the individual heat map cells. The underlying data matrix for the cell notes does not necessarily have to be the same numeric matrix we used to construct our heat map, as long as it has the same number of rows and columns.

   As we recall, the data we read from `arabidopsis_genes.csv` resembles log 2 ratios of sample and reference gene expression levels. Let us calculate the fold changes of the gene expression levels now and display them—rounded to two digits after the decimal point—as cell notes on our heat map:

```
fold_change <- 2^gene_data
rounded_fold_changes <- round(fold_change, 2)
heat2(cellnote = rounded_fold_changes,
   notecex = 0.5,
   notecol = "black",
   col = rev_heat.colors,
   main = "Cell Notes")
```

   The `notecex` parameter controls the size of the cell notes. Its default size is 1, and every argument between 0 and 1 will make the font smaller, whereas values larger than 1 will make the font larger. Here, we decreased the font size of the cell notes by 50 percent to fit it into the cell boundaries. Also, we want to display the cell notes in black to have a nice contrast to the colored background; this is controlled by the `notecol` parameter.

10. **Row and column side colors**: Another approach to pronounce certain regions, that is, rows or columns on the heat map is to make use of row and column side colors. The `ColSideColors` argument will place a colored box between the dendrogram and heat map that can be used to annotate certain columns. We pass our vector with colors to `ColSideColors`, where its length must be equal to the number of columns of the heat map. Here, we want to color the first and third column `red`, the second one `gray`, and all the remaining 13 columns `green`:

```
heat2(ColSideColors = c("red", "gray", "red", rep("green", 13)),
  main = "ColSideColors")
```

You can see in the following image how the column side colors look like when we include the `ColSideColors` argument as shown previously:

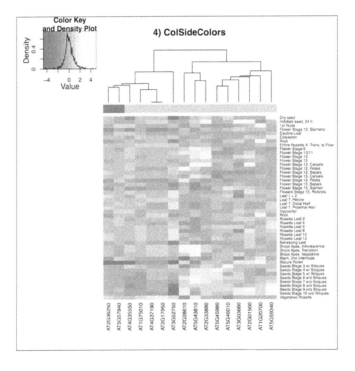

Attentive readers may have noticed that the order of colors in the column color box slightly differs from the order of colors we passed as a vector to `ColSideColors`. We see red two times next to each other, followed by a green and a gray box. This is due to the fact that the columns of our heat map have been reordered by the hierarchical clustering algorithm.

Drawing choropleth maps and contour plots (Intermediate)

We have constructed many heat maps so far, including popular applications like gene expression and stock analyses. There are many more fields and disciplines where heat maps are an invaluable tool for intuitive and data analyses and representations. In this recipe, we will learn how to construct the closely related choropleth maps and contour plots, which are very useful to visualize geographic data.

Although choropleth maps get a huge boost of popularity during the election years for sure, there are many more widely used applications, such as population census, disease factors by regions, or income comparisons. Basically, choropleth maps are the representation of choice whenever you want to show and compare statistics between geographic regions on a cartographic map. Those geographic regions are usually separated by county, state, or even country borders.

The following choropleth map shows the annual average temperatures of the US from 1971-2001:

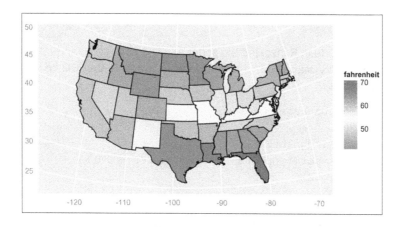

While contour plots are represented less in the media, they are extensively used by engineers and scientists. Common examples are the 2D projections of 3D surfaces, such as geographic terrains. However, contour plots have many more applications and can be used to plot gradients, depths, thicknesses, and other distributions as 2D projections.

Imagine a mountain from a bird's-eye perspective, where the contour lines delineate the different levels of altitude. The regions that are enclosed by the contour lines can be filled with colors or color gradients to better distinguish the different heights.

In the second part of this recipe, we will apply this concept by creating a contour plot of a volcano.

Getting ready

Download the `5644OS_04_01.r` script and the data files `usa_temp.csv` and `south_am_pop.csv` from your account at `http://www.packtpub.com`.

I recommend that you download and save the script and data file to the same folder on your hard drive. If you execute the script from a different location to the data file, you have to change the current R working directory accordingly.

Please read the *Getting ready* section of the *Reading data from different file formats* recipe for more information on how to change the working directory of your current R session.

For more information on how to view the current working directory of your current R session and an explanation on how to run scripts in R, please read the *Getting ready* section of the *Creating your first heat map in R* recipe.

The script will check automatically if any additional packages need to be installed in R. You can find more information about the installation of packages in the *Getting ready* section of the *Creating your first heat map in R* recipe.

How to do it...

Execute the following code in R invoking the script `5644OS_04_01.r` and take a look at the PDF files `chloropleths_maps.pdf` and `contour_plot.pdf` that will be created in the current working directory:

```
### loading packages

if (!require("ggplot2")) {
install.packages("ggplot2", dependencies = TRUE)
library(ggplot2)
}
if (!require("maps")) {
install.packages("maps", dependencies = TRUE)
library(maps)
}
if (!require("mapdata")) {
install.packages("mapdata", dependencies = TRUE)
library(mapdata)
}

pdf("chloropleth_maps.pdf", height = 7,width = 10)

### 1) average temperature USA
```

```
# 1.1) reading in and processing data
usa_map <- map_data(map = "state")

usa_temp <- read.csv("usa_temp.csv", comment.char = "#")

usa_data <- merge(usa_temp, usa_map,
by.x ="state", by.y =  "region") # case sensitive

usa_sorted <- usa_data[order(usa_data["order"]),]

# 1.2) plotting USA chloropleth maps
usa_map1 <- ggplot(data = usa_sorted) +
  geom_polygon(aes(x = long, y = lat,
group = group, fill = fahrenheit)) +
  ggtitle("USA Map 1")
print(usa_map1)

usa_map2 <- usa_map1 + coord_map("polyconic") +
  ggtitle("USA Map 2 - polyconic")
print(usa_map2)

usa_map3 <- usa_map2 +
  geom_path(aes(x = long, y = lat, group = group),
color = "black") +
  ggtitle("USA Map 3 - black contours")
print(usa_map3)

usa_map4 <- usa_map3 +
  scale_fill_gradient(low = "yellow", high = "red") +
  ggtitle("USA Map 4 - gradient 1")
print(usa_map4)

usa_map5 <- usa_map3 +
scale_fill_gradient2(low = "steelblue", mid = "yellow",
  high = "red",  midpoint = colMeans(usa_sorted["fahrenheit"])) +
  ggtitle("USA Map 5 - gradient 2")
print(usa_map5)


### 2) South American population count

# 2.1) reading in and processing data
south_am_map <- map_data("worldHires",
region = c("Argentina", "Bolivia", "Brazil",
```

```
   "Chile", "Colombia", "Ecuador", "Falkland Islands",
"French Guiana", "Guyana", "Paraguay", "Peru",
"Suriname", "Uruguay", "Venezuela"))

south_am_pop <- read.csv("south_america_pop.csv",
comment.char = "#")

south_am_data <- merge(south_am_pop, south_am_map,  by.x =
"country", by.y = "region")

south_am_sorted <- south_am_data[order(
south_am_data["order"]),]

# 2.2) creating chloropleth maps
south_am_map1 <- ggplot(data = south_am_sorted) +
  geom_polygon(aes(x = long, y = lat,
group = group, fill = population)) +
  geom_path(aes(x = long, y = lat, group = group),
color = "black") +
  coord_map("polyconic") +
scale_fill_gradient(low = "lightyellow",
  high = "red", guide = "legend")
print(south_am_map1)

south_am_map2 = south_am_map1 +
  theme(panel.background = element_blank(),
  axis.text = element_blank(),
  axis.title = element_blank(),
  axis.ticks = element_blank())
print(south_am_map2)

dev.off()


### 3) Volcano contour plot

pdf("contour_plot.pdf", height = 7,width = 10)

data(volcano)
image.plot(volcano)
contour(volcano, add = TRUE)

dev.off()
```

How it works...

In this recipe we are using three new packages that we have not encountered before. One of them is Hadley Wickham's ggplot2 package, which is a relatively new and powerful plotting system. It has become a very popular alternative to R's basic plotting functions, because it provides both great versatility and a uniform syntax. The complete documentation can be found at http://docs.ggplot2.org/current/.

The other two packages, maps and mapdata, contain the data for our maps that we are going to use as templates for our choropleth maps. You can find a table with all the maps that are available in both maps and mapdata at the end of this section.

The difference between those two map packages is that they contain different maps with different levels of detail.

The following image compares the levels of detail between the map of Japan extracted from the world map of maps, the high resolution world map of mapdata, and the single high resolution mapdata map of Japan.

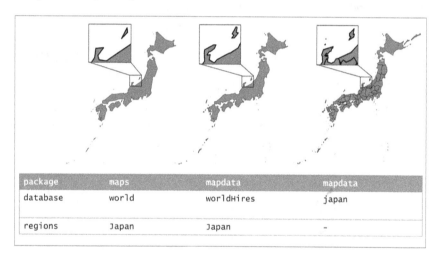

package	maps	mapdata	mapdata
database	world	worldHires	japan
regions	Japan	Japan	–

1. **Annual average temperatures of the United States**: The first data file, usa_temp. csv, contains the annual average temperatures of the USA from 1971 to 2001. The data was made available by the National Climatic Data Center of the United States, National Oceanic and Atmospheric Administration, and has been compiled by current results.

2. **Reading in map and temperature data**: First, we use the read.csv() function, known from the *Reading data from different file formats* recipe, to read our data and assign it to the variable usa_temp. Next, we use the map_data() function from the ggplot2 package to read in the United States map from maps as a data frame.

Note that in contrast to the heat map functions that we have been using in the previous recipes, the `gplot()` function takes a data frame as input instead of data in a numerical matrix format. And as we remember from the *Reading data from different file formats* recipe, data that we read via `read.csv()` is converted into a data frame automatically.

Matrices in R can only contain data of the same type, for example, numeric. However, data frames can contain different types of data as variables (columns), such as numeric, factor, logical, or character.

3. **Merging and sorting the data frames**: Now we will merge the map and temperature data:

```
usa_data <- merge(usa_temp, usa_map,
by.x = "state", by.y = "region")
usa_sorted <- usa_data[order(usa_data["order"]),]
```

The following flowchart illustrates this process and shows how the data looks like before and after the merging and conversion:

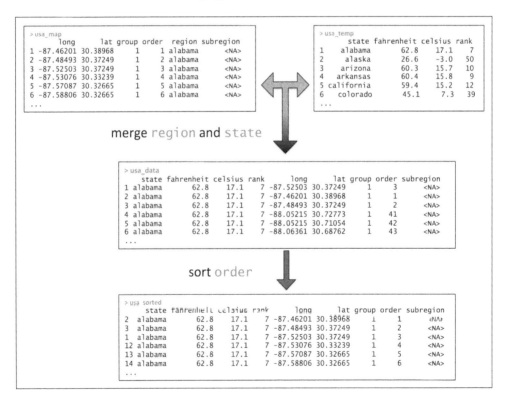

As we can see in the preceding chart, the map data in the `usa_map` data frame contains multiple longitudinal (`long`) and latitudinal (`lat`) coordinates for each state in the column labeled with region. The numbers in the order column specify the order in which the single dots are connected when we draw the map as a polygon.

After we merged both map data and temperature data, we can see that the values in the order column have been shuffled. This would result in quite a mess when we wanted to construct the choropleth map from this data frame. Therefore, we use the `order()` function to restore the original order before we merged the data sets.

The `merge()` function is case sensitive. We have to make sure that the character strings in the two columns that we want to merge match.

4. **Constructing our first choropleth map**: Now that we have our data ready in a nice format, we can proceed to the main plotting functions to create our first choropleth map:

```
usa_map1 <- ggplot(data = usa_sorted) +
  geom_polygon(aes(x = long, y = lat, group = group,
fill = fahrenheit)) +
  ggtitle("USA Map 1")
```

Basically, how the `ggplot2` package works is that we have to create our plots incrementally. First, we use the `ggplot()` function to assign our data to a new plot object, and then we can add further layers to it. The basic shape of `ggplot2` plots is determined by so-called `geoms`, or geometric objects. Here, we are using `geom_polygon()`, which will connect our coordinate points to a map. The `aes()` function nested inside is there for aesthetics and defines the visual properties of the geoms. We provide the variable `fahrenheit` as an argument for the `fill` parameter so that we can shade the areas of our choropleth maps according to the Fahrenheit temperatures in our data set.

Similar to the plotting functions of the `lattice` package, which we have used in the previous recipes, `ggplot()` creates plot graphics as objects. Therefore, we have to use the `print()` function on the objects to save them as image files. Note that in an interactive R session, you can omit the `print()` function and just need to type the name of the graphics object, for example, `usa_map1`, to create the map on the screen.

5. **Customizing choropleth maps**: One of the advantages of `ggplot2` is that we do not have to retype the whole heat map function with its arguments each time we want to modify the map, since we store our plots as objects. So if we want to convert our map into a polyconic projection, we can simple reuse our old graphic object and make a small modification:

```
usa_map2 <- usa_map1 + coord_map("polyconic") +
  ggtitle("USA Map 2 - polyconic")
```

Now, let us add another geometric object so that the state borders will be drawn as black lines:

```
usa_map3 <- usa_map2 +
  geom_path(aes(x = long, y = lat, group = group),
color = "black") +
  ggtitle("USA Map 3 - black contours")
```

Since we are showing temperatures on our United States map, it would be more appropriate to replace the blue default color gradient by a color gradient from yellow to red. We can modify the color gradient by adding the `scale_fill_gradient()` function with two color arguments for our previous graphic object:

```
usa_map4 <- usa_map3 +
  scale_fill_gradient(low = "yellow", high = "red") +
  ggtitle("USA Map 4 - gradient 1")
```

 Instead of discrete color names, we can also use the hex color codes that we have seen in the *Customizing heat maps* recipe.

If we want to add a third color to our gradient, we can use the `scale_fill_gradient2()` function instead. For this function, we need an additional argument that specifies the position (mid-point) of the second color. We can simply use the temperature mean such as a midpoint measure:

```
usa_map5 <- usa_map3 +
scale_fill_gradient2(low = "steelblue", mid = "yellow",
high = "red",  midpoint =
colMeans(usa_sorted["fahrenheit"])) +
  ggtitle("USA Map 5 - gradient 2")
```

6. **Extracting regions from the world map**: Now that we have seen how we can use `ggplot2` to create simple choropleth maps, let us explore some advanced features.

As you can see in the table at the end of this section, the number of maps in the `maps` and `mapdata` packages is quite limited. However, we are able to extract individual countries from the world map.

Our second data set, `south_am_pop.csv`, contains recent population counts of all the countries of South America. Unfortunately, neither `maps` nor `mapdata` contains a map of this continent, so we extract all the South American countries from the high resolution world map of `mapdata`.

```
south_am_map <- map_data("worldHires", region = c("Argentina",
"Bolivia", "Brazil","Chile", "Colombia", "Ecuador",
"Falkland Islands", "French Guiana", "Guyana",
"Paraguay", "Peru", "Suriname", "Uruguay", "Venezuela"))
```

After we read the data from `south_am_pop.csv` and merge and sort the data frames, we can create the choropleth map:

```
south_am_map1 <- ggplot(data = south_am_sorted) +
  geom_polygon(aes(x = long, y = lat,
group = group, fill = population)) +
  geom_path(aes(x = long, y = lat, group = group),
color = "black") +
  coord_map("polyconic") +
scale_fill_gradient(low = "lightyellow",
  high = "red", guide = "legend")
```

As we have seen it for the USA map before, we use the `ggplot()` function to create a new plot object and `geom_polygon` to construct the map graphic. With the color parameter in `geom_path`, we add a black border around the individual countries, and with the `coord_map` function, we convert our map into a polyconic projection. We also change the color gradient from light-yellow to red and make the legend categorical by providing the argument `legend` for the `guide` parameter.

By default, `ggplot2` creates plots on a gray background with a white grid. To get a nicer layout, let us create a map on a clean, white background and remove axes tick marks, labels, and titles altogether:

```
south_am_map2 = south_am_map1 +
  theme(panel.background = element_blank(),
  axis.text = element_blank(),
  axis.title = element_blank(),
  axis.ticks = element_blank())
```

In the following image, you can see the resulting choropleth map of South America's population count on a white background:

7. **Volcano contour plot**: As mentioned in the introduction of this recipe, we want to take a look at another type of map representation, **contour plots**:

```
data(volcano)
image.plot(volcano)
```

Using the `image.plot()` function from the `fields` library, we construct a color grid with the topographical data of a volcano from R's `data` package. We could also use the `image()` base function in R, but the `image.plot()` function has some nice additional features, such as placing a legend for the color grid to the right of the plot.

Aftcr wo created the underlying color grid, we use the `contour()` function to place the contour lines on top of the color grid.

```
contour(volcano, add = TRUE)
```

The following image shows the final contour plot that we have created from the `volcano` data set:

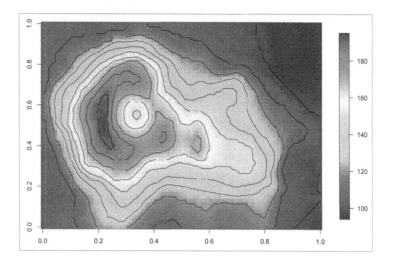

The following table summarizes the different maps that are included in the `maps` and `mapdata` packages:

Package	Database	Description
maps	usa	Map of the United States
	county	Map of the US Counties
	state	Map of the states in the US
	Italy	Map of Italy
	france	Map of France
	nz	Map of New Zealand
	world	World map
	world2	Pacific centric world map
mapdata	china	High resolution map of China
	japan	High resolution map of Japan
	nzHires	High resolution map of New Zealand
	worldHires	High resolution world map
	world2Hires	High resolution Pacific centric world map

Exporting for presentation (Simple)

After the exploratory stage of our data analyses, it is likely that we want to present our graphical heat map representations to an audience. This can be via presentation software over a projector, embedded in a website, a poster printout, or an image in a journal article. In this recipe, we will learn about the different file formats for image export so that we can choose whatever is most suited for the purpose.

Getting ready

Download the `56440S_05_01.r` script from your account at `http://www.packtpub.com` and save it to your hard drive.

For an explanation of how to run scripts in R, please read the *Getting ready* section of the *Creating your first heat map in R* recipe.

The script will check automatically if any additional packages need to be installed in R. You can find more information about the installation of packages in the *Getting ready* section of the *Creating your first heat map in R* recipe.

How to do it...

Execute the `56440S_05_01.r` script in R and compare the different image files to other that which were written to the current working directory:

```r
if (!require("gplots")) {
install.packages("gplots", dependencies = TRUE)
library(gplots)
}
if (!require("RColorBrewer")) {
install.packages("RColorBrewer", dependencies = TRUE)
library(gplots)
}

### converting data
data(co2)
rowcolNames <- list(as.character(1959:1997), month.abb)
co2_data <- matrix(co2,
  ncol = 12,
  byrow = TRUE,
  dimnames = rowcolNames)
```

```
heat2 <- function(...)
  heatmap.2(co2_data,
trace = "none",
  density.info = "none",
  dendrogram = "none",
  Colv = FALSE,
  Rowv = FALSE,
  col = colorRampPalette(c("blue", "yellow", "red")),
(n = 100),
  margin = c(5,8),
  lhei = c(0.25,1.25),
    ...)


png("1_PNG_default.png")
heat2(main = "PNG default")
dev.off()

png("2_PNG_highres.png",
  width = 5*300,
  height = 5*300,
  res = 300,
  pointsize = 8)
heat2(main = "PNG High Resolution")
dev.off()

jpeg("3_JPEG_highres.png",
  width = 5*300,
  height = 5*300,
  res = 300,
  pointsize = 8)
heat2(main = "JPEG default")
dev.off()

bmp("4_BMP_default.bmp",
width = 5*300,
  height = 5*300,
  res = 300,
  pointsize = 8)
heat2(main = "BMP default")
dev.off()

pdf("5_PDF_default.pdf",
  width = 5,
  height = 5,
  pointsize = 8)
heat2(main = "PDF default")
dev.off()
```

```
svg("6_SVG_default.svg",
  width = 5,
  height = 5,
  pointsize = 8)
heat2(main = "SVG default")
dev.off()

svg("7_PostScript_default.ps",
  width = 5,
  height = 5,
  pointsize = 8)
heat2(main = "PostScript default")
dev.off()

png("8_PNG_transp.png",
  width = 5*300,
  height = 5*300,
  res = 300,
  pointsize = 8,
  bg = "transparent")
heat2(main = "PNG Transparent Background")
dev.off()

pdf("9_PDF_mono.pdf",
  family = "Courier",
  paper = "USr")
heat2(main = "PDF Monospace Font")
dev.off()
```

How it works...

There are two major classes of image formats that we can choose from when we want to save our plots as a file: **vector graphics** and **raster graphics**. Raster graphics, also known as **bitmaps**, comprise popular image formats such as PNG, BMP, and JPEG. These file formats store information of each individual pixel, thus the quality of the image heavily depends on the resolution, that is **pixel per inch** (**ppi**). However, high-resolution images come with the additional cost of a large file size. Nowadays, we usually do not have to worry about limited storage space of a hard drive anymore, but large images are not suitable for the Web, and in the worst case, they can also have a negative impact on the responsiveness of your presentation software.

One of the nice features of R is to save plots as vector graphics, such as SVG, PDF, and **PostScript**. While all three vector graphic formats offer high quality graphics, each has its own area of application. SVG can be easily embedded into HTML code and is the format of choice for displaying your plots on the Web. PostScript is the desired format when you want to send articles to a journal, where as PDF is well known for its great compatibility with a wide range of software including PDF readers.

 If you are interested to see how the SVG and PostScript code looks like, I encourage you to open the SVG and PostScript files that were created by this script in your favorite plain text editor (for example, TextEdit on Mac OS X or Notepad on Windows).

Rather than storing information of each pixel in a grid, vector graphic files contain instructions for geometrical shapes that are used by the visualization software to render the image. This allows us to zoom in to the image without any loss of quality. Another advantage of vector images is that they generally have a much smaller file size than raster graphics. The only exception is when your plot is heavily over-plotted, so that a lot of instructions have to be saved in the vector graphic file. Generally, vector graphics are great to store image files on your computer, however images can only be rendered by certain software and are converted to raster graphics for printing.

Images from SVG files, for example, can be rendered in every modern web browser, and since they are saved as **Extensible Markup Language** (**XML**) code, they can be easily embedded into HTML, which makes SVG the format of choice if you want to display your graphics on a website.

If you do not consider to embed your graphic in a website or send your graphics off to a journal for professional publication, I recommend using the PDF format, since it has great compatibility with other software and offers best quality output in reasonably small file sizes.

You will find an overview table of the different graphic devices that are available in R at the end of this section.

Now let us dive in and create different image files from our heat maps:

1. **Reading data**: For this recipe, we will use the co2 data set from the data package in R. This co2 data set is a time-series that consists of 468 monthly measurements of **carbon dioxide** (**CO2**) concentrations in **parts per million** (**ppm**) from 1959 to 1997.

   We know from the *Creating your first heat map in R* recipe how to convert data from a time-series format into a numeric matrix, which is the only format that is compatible with the heatmap2.() function.

2. **Setting up our own heatmap.2() function**: Like we did in the *Customizing heat maps* recipe, we create our own derivative of the `heatmap.2()` function with some default arguments that we want to use for all our heat maps in this recipe to avoid repetitive typing efforts:

```
heat2 <- function(...)
  heatmap.2(co2_data,
trace = "none",
  density.info = "none",
  dendrogram = "none",
  Colv = FALSE,
  Rowv = FALSE,
  col = colorRampPalette(c("blue", "yellow", "red")),
(n = 100),
  margin = c(5,8),
  lhei = c(0.25,1.25),
   ...)
```

We use a new parameter `lhei` that we have not encountered so far. With this parameter, we can control the height of the different plot elements. The arguments we provide here will make our legend thinner.

Before we proceed with the graphic devices, let us briefly take a look at the general paradigm of creating image files in R, which consists of three basic steps as follows:

1. Opening a graphics device.

2. Calling a plotting function.

3. Closing the graphics device.

3. **Creating image files**: First, let us create a PNG file using the `png()` function with its default parameters:

```
png("1_PNG_default.png")
heat2(main = "PNG default")
dev.off()
```

The first argument that the graphics device takes is the name of the output file. After we open the graphics device, we create the heat map using our `heat2()` function, and lastly, we close the graphic device with the `dev.off()` function.

Very often, the main reason why we cannot open a PDF file that we created in R is that we forgot to close the PDF graphics device after we finished plotting!

Because the resolution of the PNG image is very low (75 ppi) when we use `png()` with its default parameters, we create another PNG file with a resolution of 300 ppi, which should provide reasonable quality for a print out on a letter-sized piece of paper. The default size of `png()` is measured in pixels, and here we are creating a 5 x 5 inches output by taking the number of pixels per inch and multiplying it by 5 inches. Further, we decrease the text size slightly from 12 to 8 bp (1 bp equals 1/72 inches) in the `pointsize` parameter:

```
png("2_PNG_highres.png",
  width = 5*300,
  height = 5*300,
  res = 300,
  pointsize = 8)
heat2(main = "PNG High Resolution")
dev.off()
```

Next, we create a JPEG, BMB, SVG, and PDF file with the same parameters so we can compare them to each other. Note that the height and width of the SVG and PDF files are measured in inches.

 You do not have to download special software to view the SVG file. Simply open it in your favorite web browser.

When we compare those different image files to each other, we see that they all show the same heat map, but if we zoom in, we notice that the quality differs tremendously.

 The difference between JPEG, PNG, and BMP is that BMP stores the image file without compression, PNG with lossless compression, and JPEG with a lossy compression, respectively.

In the following image, you can see the tremendous difference in the image quality between the different file formats. This is something you should consider, especially if you are preparing your graphics for an on-screen presentation.

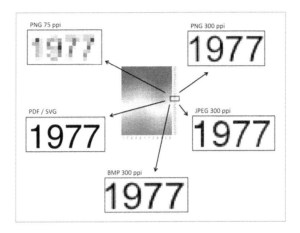

When we view the BMP, PNG, and JPEG images, the quality seems to be quite reasonable. But as soon as we zoom in on the image, we can barely read the text of the PNG file with the 75 ppi default. In contrast to the 300 ppi BMP, PNG and JPEG files do not have any jagged edges in the PDF and SVG files, no matter how far we zoom in.

Of course, we can increase the ppi amount of the raster graphics even further, however it depends on the purpose of the image and where it will be presented.

4. **More options**: So if we have the choice between the different raster graphics formats, I recommend using PNG, since the files are way smaller then BMP files due to the lossless compression. Using JPEG over PNG should only be considered if file size really matters to you.

In contrast to JPEG files, BMP and PNG files support transparent backgrounds. This is particularly useful if we want to place the heat map on a patterned background, on a poster, or a presentation slide for example. This can be specified by providing the argument `transparent` for the `bg` (background) parameter.

Similarly, we could also use a color name instead of `transparent` to create a colored background.

```
png("test/8_PNG_transp.png",
  width = 5*300,
  height = 5*300,
  res = 300,
  pointsize = 8,
  bg = "transparent")
heat2(main = "PNG Transparent Background")
dev.off()
```

 The background of the image files in PDF format is transparent by default.

The PDF format has the further advantage wherein we can choose a different font family if we like. We can choose from AvantGarde, Bookman, Courier, Helvetica, Helvetica-Narrow, NewCenturySchoolbook, Palatino, and Times. Also, we can specify the paper format, such as a4 for **DIN A4**, letter for the **American Standard Letter** format, or a4r and USr for the respective rotated landscape formats:

```
pdf("9_PDF_mono.pdf",
  family = "Courier",
  paper = "USr")
heat2(main = "PDF Monospace Font")
dev.off()
```

The following table shows the different graphic devices that are available in R:

On-screen devices		
	x11()	X Window System (X11), default in Unix/Linux
	quartz()	Quartz, default on Mac OS X
	windows()	Default in Microsoft Windows
Raster graphics devices		
	jpeg()	**Joint Photographics Experts Group** (**JPEG**) image file with lossy compression
	png()	**Portable Network Graphics** (**PNG**) image file with lossless compression
	bmp()	**Bitmap** (**BMP**) image file with no compression
	tiff()	**Tagged Image File Format** (**TIFF**) with optional compression

Vector image devices		
	`pdf()`	Adobe's popular **Portable Documents Format** (**PDF**)
	`svg()`	XML-based **Scalable Vector Graphics** (**SVG**) format
	`postscript()`	**PostScript** (**PS**) format
Other		
	`xfig()`	File format for **Xfig vector graphics editor**
	`pictex()`	Graphics format for **LaTex** import

Bringing your data to life (Advanced)

We learned how to create heat maps, customize them, and save them as image files. Now, it is time to go a step further and add some interactivity for displaying them on the Web. In this recipe, we will learn how to manipulate heat map-containing SVG files to add a nice hover effect and fade-in tool tips using CSS. Further, we will see how to embed our heat map in HTML files, and make use of JavaScript to add further interactivity.

The following screenshot was captured from a Safari web browser after applying the hover effect to our SVG image. Notice the highlighted cell under the mouse pointer:

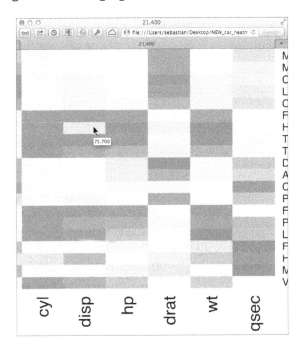

Getting ready

Download the 5644OS_06_01.r script and a version of the HeatModSVG program for your operating system from your account at http://www.packtpub.com. It is recommended, but not mandatory, to download the latest version of the svgpan JavaScript library from, by Andrea Leofreddi, https://code.google.com/p/svgpan/downloads/list.

Further, I recommend that you save all files to the same folder on your computer.

For an explanation on how to run scripts in R, please read the *Getting ready* section of the *Creating your first heat map in R* recipe.

The script will check automatically if any additional packages need to be installed in R. You can find more information about the installation of packages in the *Getting ready* section of the *Creating your first heat map in R* recipe.

How to do it...

Run the 5644OS_06_01.r script and then launch HeatModSVG (see the instructions below the script contents):

```
if (!require("gplots")) {
install.packages("gplots", dependencies = TRUE)
library(gplots)
}
if (!require("MASS")) {
install.packages("MASS", dependencies = TRUE)
library(MASS)
}

# Writing out matrix file
data(mtcars)
car_data <- mtcars[,1:7]
write.matrix(car_data, "car_data.csv", sep = ",")
norm_cars <- scale(car_data) # automatically matrix

# Creating heat map
svg("car_heatmap.svg")
heatmap.2(norm_cars,
   density.info = "none",
   trace = "none",
   dendrogram = "none",
   Rowv = FALSE,
   Colv = FALSE,
   margin = c(5,10))

dev.off()
```

After you have ran the R script, make sure that two new files were created in the current working directory: `car_heatmap.svg` and `car_data.csv`. Now, double-click on the `HeatModSVG` program and a new window should appear on your screen. The lines that require your input are highlighted in the sample session as follows. You can just take over the inputs of this sample session, but make sure that you type in the correct location of the `car_heatmap.svg` heat map file and the `car_data.csv` data file.

```
####################################
##                                ##
## HeatModSVG v 1.06 (04/04/2013)  ##
##                                ##
## Written by Sebastian Raschka    ##
##                                ##
####################################



===============
=== Options ===
===============

-- Add Tool Tips: t
-- Add Zoom and Panning: z
-- Add Both: tz
-- Quit: q

Enter your choice: tz
Current working directory: /Users/sebastian
SVG file: /Users/sebastian/Desktop/car_heatmap.svg
Matrix file: /Users/sebastian/Desktop/car_data.csv



MATRIX SPECIFICATION
--------------------


Comment character: #

Separator
-- "w" for whitespace
-- "t" for tab
-- "c" for comma
: c
Column names? (y/n): y
Row names? (y/n): n
```

```
Read in data from car_data.csv:


21.000  6.000    160.000 110.000 3.900    2.620    16.460
21.000  6.000    160.000 110.000 3.900    2.875    17.020
22.800  4.000    108.000 93.000  3.850    2.320    18.610
...
21.400  4.000    121.000 109.000 4.110    2.780    18.600
```

Add a label to tool tips? (y/n): n

```
... inserted CSS <style> tag after line 2

... inserted link to svgPan.js after CSS <style> tag

... added viewport ID in line 286

... IDs and tool tip <title> tags were inserted in lines 289 to 512

Saving . . . . . . . .

==> Created /Users/sebastian/Desktop/NEW_car_heatmap.svg
```

How it works...

To add interactivity to our heat maps, we will make use of R's capability to store the created images in the Scalable Vector Graphics format. The content of SVG files is saved as plain text and can be viewed with any text editor. If we open an SVG file in a text editor, we will see XML code that contains the information for our web browser to render the image.

The advantage of this XML code is that we can manipulate it using HTML, CSS, and JavaScript.

1. **Creating a heat map SVG file in R**: First, we create our heat map by running the R script 5644OS_06_01.r. By now, the contents of the script should look very familiar to us, but let us go over it briefly.

   We create our heat map from the mtcars data set from the R data package. The data set contains information about 32 car models from 1973-1974. The data columns from 1 to 7 contain information on miles per gallon, number of cylinders, displacement in cubic inches, horsepower, rear axle ratio, weight (lb/1000), and one fourth mile time.

   ```
   data(mtcars)
   car_data <- mtcars[,1:7]
   write.matrix(car_data, "car_data.csv", sep = ",")
   ```

Using the `write.matrix()` function, we add the `mtcars` data in a CSV file. We will need this data file later to add tool tips to our heat map.

We use the `scale()` function to normalize the data, so we can compare the different variables of `mtcars` to each other in the heat map. Note that `mtcars` is in a data frame format, but `scale()` will automatically convert it into a numerical matrix. Finally, we open a new graphic device to save our heat map to an SVG file.

```
norm_cars <- scale(car_data)

# Creating heat map
svg("car_heatmap.svg")
heatmap.2(norm_cars,
  density.info = "none",
  trace = "none",
  dendrogram = "none",
  Rowv = FALSE,
  Colv = FALSE,
  margin = c(5,10))

dev.off()
```

2. **HeatModSVG options overview**: Now that we have created an SVG file of our heat map, we can use the `HeatModSVG` program to add some interactivity to it. Let us take a look at the execution of the program before we discuss how it modifies the SVG file in more detail.

   First, the program asks us whether we want to add **Tool Tips** or **Zoom and Panning** or both. When we choose both, the program will insert tool tip labels from an external data file that will be displayed in the individual heat map cells when we hover over it with the mouse pointer. Further, the program will embed a reference to Andrea Leofreddi's `SVGPan` JavaScript library, which will add features like zooming, dragging, and panning to our heat map.

3. **Reading a data file into HeatModSVG**: To add tool tips to our heat map, the `HeatModSVG` program will prompt us for a data file in addition to the SVG file that we want to modify.

   This tool tip label data can stem from the same data file that we used to create our heat map, or it can be another text file that contains data with the same dimensions (a similar number of rows and columns like the heat map data file).

   In our case, we want to show the original values of the `mtcars` columns from 1 to 7 that we saved to `car_data.csv` before we normalize the data to create the heat map.

The following screenshot highlights the important formatting features of the `car_data.csv` file that we have to feed into the `HeatModSVG` program:

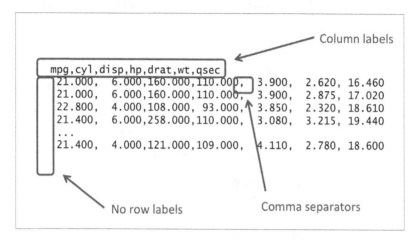

The `HeatModSVG` program will ask us for the format of the comment characters in the data file, so it can ignore those lines when it reads the data. We entered #, but in the case of `car_data.csv`, it does not really matter, since `car_data.csv` does not contain any comments.

Next, we chose c (comma) as the column separator, since we created `car_data.csv` as a Comma Separated Value file in R. When `HeatModSVG` asks us for row labels, we choose no, and for column names, we choose yes, since `car_data.csv` only has a header and no row labels.

After we have specified all these options `HeatModSVG` prompted us to make, the contents of the data file will be printed to the screen based on how it was read in by `HeatModSVG`. This is the point where we should double-check whether we provided the correct options to `HeatModSVG` for reading in the data file—we should only see the matrix values here and no row and column labels.

Finally, the program will ask us if we want to add a label that will be placed in front of our tool tips. If we would have chosen yes, we would have been prompted to enter a character or character string that will appear as a global label in front of our tool tip values, and the tool tips would then be displayed in the following format: `<Label:>` `<value>`.

Just before the program finishes, it will notify us about the changes that it made to the original SVG file:

```
... inserted CSS <style> tag after line 2

... inserted link to svgPan.js after CSS <style> tag
```

```
... added viewport ID in line 286

... IDs and tool tip <title> tags were inserted in lines 289
    to 512

Saving . . . . . . . .

==> Created /Users/sebastian/Desktop/NEW_car_heatmap.svg
```

4. **Modification to the SVG file**: Let us take a look at the changes made by
   `HeatModSVG` step-by-step to understand how the interactivity effect works:

```
... inserted CSS <style> tag after line 2
```

When we open the new SVG file, `NEW_car_heatmap.svg`, we see that the program
inserted a CSS style tag just after line 2:

```
<style>
#hoverItem:hover{opacity: 0.3;}
</style>
```

This CSS style tag adds a mouse-over or hover effect to each element in the XML file
that we label with the CSS ID `hoverItem`.

Next, a link to the `SVGPan.js` JavaScript file was inserted at the top of the SVG file,
right after the previously inserted CSS style tag:

```
... inserted link to svgPan.js after CSS <style> tag
```

The link to the JavaScript file looks like this:

```
<script xlink:href="SVGPan.js"/>
```

In order for `svgpan` to work, it has to be in the same folder as the SVG file, or else
we have to add the path in front of it.

Alternatively, you can also copy the complete contents of `SVGPan.js`
into your SVG file script tags:

```
<script> SVGPan.js contents </script>
```

In order for the `SVGPan` effects to work, we have to add the ID `viewport` to the heat
map elements:

```
... added viewport ID in line 286
```

Note that the number 286 refers to the location in the original SVG file; since we
inserted four lines already, we will find the `viewport` ID opening tag in line 290
of the new SVG file:

```
<g id="viewport">.
```

In fact, `viewport` replaced another ID, `surface61`; this is the ID that determines the start of the visual elements of our heat map.

 The contents of the SVG file might seem very confusing. To get an idea about its structure and how it is structured, I recommend you to simply find it out by deleting individual elements from the XML code and see how the SVG image changes in the browser.

At this point, you may ask why we need an extra program to make those tiny changes to the XML code. In fact, we could have done everything manually in no time, but stay tuned, because now comes the laborious part:

```
... IDs and tool tip <title> tags were inserted in lines 289 to
512
```

At the beginning, we saw the CSS style tag that contained the hover action added in line number 3. Now, we have to assign it to each individual cell of the heat map by adding the `hoverItem` ID. Further, we want to add the tool tip label from the `car_data.csv` file to these cells too, so that a value appears if we hover over a particular cell in the heat map.

Without a program to automate this process, we would have to repeat this process 224 times to add the `hoverItem` ID and tool tip label to each cell of the 32 x 7 heat map.

The following screenshot shows an XML that shows how an exemplary heat map cell looks like before and after the conversion:

`car_heatmap.svg`:

```
<path style=" stroke:none;fill-rule:nonzero;fill:rgb(100%,43.137255%,0%);fill-
opacity:1;" d="M 137.453125 434.652344 L 172.742188 434.652344 L 172.742188
425.066406 L 137.453125 425.066406 Z "/>
```

`NEW_car_heatmap.svg`:

```
<g><title>21.400</title>
<path style=" stroke:none;fill-rule:nonzero;fill:rgb(100%,89.019608%,0%);fill-
opacity:1;" d="M 137.453125 444.238281 L 172.742188 444.238281 L 172.742188
434.652344 L 137.453125 434.652344 Z " id = "hoverItem"/>
</g>
```

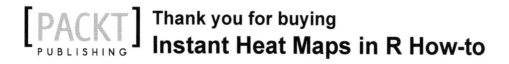

Thank you for buying
Instant Heat Maps in R How-to

About Packt Publishing

Packt, pronounced 'packed', published its first book "*Mastering phpMyAdmin for Effective MySQL Management*" in April 2004 and subsequently continued to specialize in publishing highly focused books on specific technologies and solutions.

Our books and publications share the experiences of your fellow IT professionals in adapting and customizing today's systems, applications, and frameworks. Our solution based books give you the knowledge and power to customize the software and technologies you're using to get the job done. Packt books are more specific and less general than the IT books you have seen in the past. Our unique business model allows us to bring you more focused information, giving you more of what you need to know, and less of what you don't.

Packt is a modern, yet unique publishing company, which focuses on producing quality, cutting-edge books for communities of developers, administrators, and newbies alike. For more information, please visit our website: www.packtpub.com.

Writing for Packt

We welcome all inquiries from people who are interested in authoring. Book proposals should be sent to author@packtpub.com. If your book idea is still at an early stage and you would like to discuss it first before writing a formal book proposal, contact us; one of our commissioning editors will get in touch with you.

We're not just looking for published authors; if you have strong technical skills but no writing experience, our experienced editors can help you develop a writing career, or simply get some additional reward for your expertise.

Circos Data Visualization How-to [Instant]

ISBN: 978-1-84969-440-7   Paperback: 72 pages

Create dynamic data visualizations in the social, physical, and computer sciences with the Circos data visualization program

1. Learn something new in an Instant! A short, fast, focused guide delivering immediate results.

2. Transform simple tables into engaging diagrams

3. Learn to install Circos on Windows, Linux, and MacOS

4. Create Circos diagrams using ribbons, heatmaps, and other data tracks

MATLAB Graphics and Data Visualization Cookbook

ISBN: 978-1-84969-316-5   Paperback: 284 pages

Tell data stories with compelling graphics using this collection of data visualization recipes

1. Collection of data visualization recipes with functionalized versions of common tasks for easy integration into your data analysis workflow

2. Recipes cross-referenced with MATLAB product pages and MATLAB Central File Exchange resources for improved coverage

3. Includes hand created indices to find exactly what you need; such as application driven, or functionality driven solutions

Please check **www.PacktPub.com** for information on our titles

Data Visualization: a successful design process

ISBN: 978-1-84969-346-2   Paperback: 206 pages

A structured design approach to equip you with the knowledge of how to successfully accomplish any data visualization challenge efficiently and effectively

1. A portable, versatile and flexible data visualization design approach that will help you navigate the complex path towards success

2. Explains the many different reasons for creating visualizations and identifies the key parameters which lead to very different design options

3. Thorough explanation of the many visual variables and visualization taxonomy to provide you with a menu of creative options

Tableau Data Visualization Cookbook

ISBN: 978-1-84968-978-6   Paperback: 200 pages

Over 70 recipes for creating visual stories with your data using Tableau

1. Quickly create impressive and effective graphics which would usually take hours in other tools

2. Lots of illustrations to keep you on track

3. Includes examples that apply to a general audience

Please check **www.PacktPub.com** for information on our titles

www.ingramcontent.com/pod-product-compliance
Lightning Source LLC
Chambersburg PA
CBHW060205060326
40690CB00018B/4263